The Family Legacy Journal

Written by Claire Ellen for
THEARCHERSWAY.COM

Copyright © 2024 by Claire Ellen

All rights reserved. No part of this book may be used or reproduced by any means, graphic, electronic, or mechanical, including photocopying, recording, taping, or by any information storage retrieval system, without the written permission of the publisher except in the case of brief quotations embodied in critical articles and reviews.

Edited by Erica Harris @ericathebraveministries
Inspired by the joys and challenges of everyday family life and a desire to raise people of integrity, kindness and compassion.

Welcome to a new year in your Family's legacy!

The Archer's Way is dedicated to supporting, encouraging and inspiring intentional families to create a legacy that lasts. It is about seeing families thrive, build deep connections and find joy in each other through all seasons of family life.

This book is intended to assist you in creating the habits, culture and traditions you have always envisioned or believed for in your family.

Within these pages you will find prompts to help you identify your vision and map your path to success. There are pages to aid you to set achievable goals. Pages for you to document the necessary actions required to meet these goals and keep a record of your success for future reference.

I hope one day you will be able to look over your bookshelf, lined with **The Archer's Way Legacy Journal's**, and be reminded of your commitment to an intentional family culture and household and know that you built a legacy that lasts.

Contents

A Little Bit About Me… 1

Why Use a Family Legacy Journal 6

How to Make Entries 9

How Often Do I Need to Revisit my Entries? 14

My Family/Household Strengths 16

Core Fears…yes, we do need to talk about it 20

Core Visions: H/O/M/E 23

Daily Affirmation List 284

Moments that are Memories to Keep… 286

Calendar to Mark Milestones 288

Books, Resources and Notable Quotes 301

Notes 303

A Little Bit About Me…

"Be the change you wish to see in the world"

- Gandi

Hi,

My name is Claire and I'm so glad you have picked up this book and are looking to create your intentional and curated family legacy. I'd like to tell you some of my story to help you understand why this is so important to me and why I believe that this is one of the most important investments you will ever make.

I live on a small homestead near Adelaide, Australia. Being able to enjoy the beauty of life here fills my soul with joy. The long shadows of dusk stretching over the land as I walk through the pastures feeding the cows. The soft, early light streaming through the window over the sink and dancing across my kitchen table at breakfast. The smell winter campfires and the familiar comfort of sausages sizzling on a bbq. I love it all!!!

I live with my husband of 20 years and my 5 homeschooled children (and the house cow Valerie). We are part of a thriving local community where we find deep connections, inspiration and belonging. I love my days at home with my children and sharing chores and coffee with my husband.

But this life didn't just happen all by itself, it has taken years of dedication to assessing and reassessing what makes our family thrive, what builds and what tears down.

As a young adult I studied psychology and psychotherapy and pursued work in High Schools as a counselor. Many of the children I worked with were seriously disadvantaged and had daily struggles both at school and home. I was passionate about seeing each of my clients turn a corner and desire a better outcome for their lives than what had been laid before them. I loved every minute of it and was highly motivated to pursue a career in psychotherapy. Seeing young people make good choices and work towards a rewarding future has always been a passion of mine and to this day, I will take every opportunity to speak into the lives of those young people around me.

I married the man of my dreams when we were still in college/university (after meeting each other only 8 months earlier)!! Talk about a baptism of fire! Joining two very different people from very different backgrounds did not result in the matrimonial bliss we had pictured for ourselves. We were so passionately in love and sure of our future together that we had taken little time to consider the consequences of having such different families of origin and belief structures.

Everything from attitudes to finances, traditions and special occasions, desires for a family and even how to have a fight were polar opposites for us! This was a hard season, but having committed "till death do us part", we knew we had to navigate a way through.

And what we realised in amongst all the argy bargy of life, is that we were unified in some very foundational things. Our faith in Jesus was and is the backbone to our connection and our commitment to follow His leading is the map we have used to navigate our journey. This meant we could set goals or targets that we agreed upon and that we felt were inspired by our faith in Jesus.

We both agreed upon the destination, it turns out we just had very different ideas about how to get there. My husband and I developed a practice of setting vision for our lives which we revisited annually to reassess. This vision was to do with finances, relationships, starting a family, skills we wished to learn and so much more.

By taking this approach we achieved a great deal more than we would have if we had just allowed each day to evolve on its own. Furthermore, we were able to reflect on how our vision changed with time, what became more important and what became less so, what we felt led to and away from. We could feel a sense of togetherness even when our paths did not always cross that often. This also gave us a framework to decide how we spent our time, money and resources by assessing how each of these things fit or didn't fit into our vision framework.

In our 20 years of marriage we have achieved more than I thought possible! We have paid off the mortgage on two homes, started, scaled and sold our own company, learnt to farm and create a sustainable homestead for better health, grown significantly in our spiritual lives and are raising and homeschooling five generous, considerate and confident young people.

Please don't read this and think that we were born high achievers! I am not a type A personality and do not always enjoy choosing to be so structured, I really do love and value a "go with the flow" lifestyle. However, I have also learned that what feels good, isn't always good for us. We also have our own family struggles with relationships, health and neurodiversity just like everyone else. Yet, by using *The Archer's Way* system, I have learned to live with all our quirks and uniqueness within a framework that still archives our vision for the week, year and ultimately our family legacy.

When I reflect on the things we've done well, I can see the pattern of repeat visioning and subsequent achieving. When I reflect on the areas we haven't done as well in our marriage, family, health and finances, I can see that we never set a clear vision and this explains not only the stress in these areas, but also the deficit. It isn't always easy and often times we would prefer to stick our heads in the sand and just accept the daily chaos, stress or disappointment as "the way it is". I still catch myself doing this sometimes.

But what if we could be living our vision in all areas of our lives without feeling strain? Would this lead to less stress, more connection and more energy to spend on the things that matter? Most definitely! Which is why I have written this book for my own family and also for yours.

a note about faith: This book is written for everyone, all families no matter your faith decisions. Our family depends heavily on impartations from the Holy Spirit to guide us towards which vision to sow and lean into. If you would like to discuss this further, please get in touch via the "contact" page at thearchersway.com

However, this book is a tool for all parents and families to build connection and legacy regardless of your faith decision as all families need intentional vision in order to thrive.

Why Use a Family Legacy Journal

"Existence flows past us like a river..."

— Marcus Aurelius

Welcome to a new season in your life! A season in which you are going to move into new levels of connection with your family! A season in which you are going to start thinking about and then implementing your vision driven initiatives in your household to bring joy, connection and purpose to all in your family.

In this season you will become more intentional in the many areas of family life, you will also feel less stress as decisions become easier to make when you see them through the framework of this intentional, vision setting strategy. As you lay down this framework, you will find peace and clarity, knowing in your heart where you are heading today, next week and in the future. I hope that one day, many years from now, you will look back on these precious years raising a family and think "I did that well!"

So...am I offering you a magic button solution that will suddenly see you flirting with your spouse, adoring your children and going to bed each night feeling like a boss? No, not really...

Is this going to be hard at first, a little confronting and maybe feel like it's not working at times? Yes!

Yet, is this going to be life changing, future altering and help you develop the family connection and household you have longed for? YES!

There is no turning back now, so let's get right into it!

So, why would you use a Family Legacy Journal?

Almost 2000 years ago, Marcus Aurelius said that "existence flows past us like a river" and that is no less true today. Too often we wake each day and go about our habitual tasks, mundane chores, relationships and work on autopilot, doing what needs to be done without much thought for it. It is all too easy to just exist each day with all the stressors, pressures and busyness of family life.

Rarely do we have the time or opportunity to sit back and take stock of what is happening in the very fibres of our household. What are the patterns and habits we have developed? How do we relate to each other? What traditions do we have? What cultural norms do we practice?

Whether we think about it or not, each family is creating a legacy, something that will be the foundations for our children's future and the memories of their past. We may not be intentional in choosing them, and yet, they exist. And our lives flow past us like a river, each moment never to be within our grasp again. Suddenly it's the end of another day, week or year.

Suddenly our babies are out of diapers, our teen is learning to drive or our young adult is moving out. And we are left to reflect on time gone by. Were we good stewards of that time? Did we teach them enough? How did we model our marriage? What did we teach them about how to treat others? Did we create enough time to play or laugh or cry together?

It is not okay to simply *hope* that you've done enough or to *wish* that these things will work out in the end. What we know about raising children in the 21st Century is that there is plenty out there that will get in the way of them becoming all that they could be. Knowing that what we sow we will reap is never truer than it is today.

Life is so busy and there is so much grabbing our children's attention and influencing their impressionable developing minds. We do not have the luxury of simply hoping it will all be ok. We, as the parents in the household, need to sow good seeds everyday so that one day, the harvest will be plentiful.

An old proverb tells us that "children are like arrows in the hands of a warrior, blessed is he who has a quiver full of them".

As parents, we are to be just like an Archer taking aim: we are to shoot straight and true in order to hit our target of raising children of integrity and honor.

How to Make Entries

"If you didn't write it down, it didn't happen."

This journal has the capacity to be as helpful as you make it. This is your life after all so give it your absolute best! The Journal is broken down in 4 core categories for family lifeWhy do we use 4 categories when this journal is intended to assist you in creating greater connection and family legacy? The reason is simple. How can we expect to succeed in building deep, fulfilling family connections when we are tired, sore, distracted, overwhelmed or stressed about finances.

Our bodies are the powerhouse to our success and need looking after. Our minds are the garden where our attitudes and intentions grow. And our production or endeavor (finances, work, play) can give us the stability and freedom to focus on those we love.

Journal Categories- H / O / M / E

H stands for Head and Heart.

This section is for your spiritual or mental vision. You will document anything regarding faith, mental health, mindfulness, spirituality or personal development. This section can often be overlooked but is *crucial* to you creating a balanced and healthy family.

O stands for Others.

This is where you will document how you are planning to increase connection and intimacy in your family. This may relate to your spouse or partner, children, extended family, church or community. This is for all your *relationship* visions.

M stands for Movement and Metabolism.

You got it, everything to do with health and wellness goes here. It is vital to move and eat well. To have health goals not only for your own body but also to *model* to your children.

E stands for Endeavour.

This is your production and it might be your work, business or study. It could also be your home making or homeschooling. It could be your artwork or a volunteer role. This is your endeavor in life and is something you are passionate about or spend significant time *investing* in each week.

On each page you will find a space to write a general vision, a big picture concept. You might write "communicate better with my partner."This is such a necessary and beautiful goal. Spending time thinking and planning about how to enjoy your spouse and understand each other better is a worthy goal. However, this vision alone will not come to much as it is so general it can feel unattainable.

Which is why, further down the page in the **PLAN IT** section you will find a space to get really specific about this vision - what would that look like, feel like, sound like? What would you be doing daily or weekly to achieve this goal?

There are also monthly and weekly pages to break it down into actions that can be tracked.

I am going to work through some examples below to give you a guide on how to make this book as effective as it can be. If you can apply this blueprint, you will be soaring!

For example, mapping the vision above might be; "to have a weekly date night" or " to put our devices away when talking with each other" or "to practice reflective listening when in a disagreement".

Be as specific as you can and write down any potential blockages to getting this done - eg: "book babysitter in advance" should be written down here to ensure a lack of babysitter doesn't prevent you achieving this plan.

It might seem silly to write down such seemingly simple things, however, NOT writing it down can be the biggest reason it doesn't happen.

We will work through another example to make sure the pattern is clear.

General vision: To be fit and healthy.

What an important goal, we all want to live long and productive lives. We all need to care for our bodies and invest in them so they can go the distance. This general vision can be really difficult to achieve though as it's very broad and doesn't help you know what to do next.

In the **PLAN IT** section, you can take the time to really think about what you need to do to achieve this goal.

PLAN IT: Walk 2x per week around the neighborhood.

Only drink alcohol on weekends, etc.

Note on **PLAN IT** section:

I say to my children, "How do you eat an elephant? You eat it one bite at a time!"

It is impossible to eat an elephant in one sitting - but it is possible to eat an elephant one small part at a time.

Why is this relevant? Because it's not helpful for you to set an elephant sized goal in the **PLAN IT** area.

There is no point deciding you are going to hit the gym 5x per week and deadlift 100kg if you do not currently have a gym habit. There is no one out there eating that elephant all at once!

But to take the first bite… that's doable! Think about setting a goal that is just one bite of that elephant. If you are already running each day, could you run further? Or in a faster time? If you are trying to lose weight, could you lose 1kg this week? If you do not yet have an exercise routine, could you add in a ½ hr walk on Sundays?

Set a vision and plan that is specific and achievable and you WILL be able to achieve bit.

It is important that these plans are specific - you need to see them like a checklist, something you can mark off as done. Eventually, you will notice that your *General Visions* have also been achieved, through pursuing smaller more specific plans that are achievable.

Set your target 1 step ahead of where you are currently and before you know it you will have eaten the whole elephant! You will be at the gym 5x per week or eating the diet you desire, or enjoying a fulfilling connection with your child or spouse. It really is that simple and achievable and I know you can do it!

It is also important to know that this is YOUR journal, documenting YOUR family goals. You can use every page and question, or only the ones you feel are relevant to you. There is no FAILING here!! You have chosen to invest in a *Family Legacy Journal* to develop your family's culture and connection so every step you take now is going to land you in a better place than you were before. This is a resource designed for YOU.

How Often Do I Need to Revisit my Entries?

The Archer's Way Family Legacy Journal is broken down into three sections.

ANNUAL VISION

Your annual vision is for your blue sky or bigger picture goals. It is here you will set visions or plans that reflect your direction as a family. Who do you want to be? What are your family characteristics? What habits, traditions and connections do you want to establish?

These visions may be inspired by your faith, resources you've engaged in or things you've always dreamed of. Really take the time to think on these and paint a picture of the family legacy you desire to build. I would suggest a date night and some conversation with your partner to make sure you are on the same page. Make this an annual night out together to set up for the new year in unity.

90 DAY PLAN

Once you have set your big picture vision, the next stage is to break it down into achievable milestones in the 90 day breakdown. Breaking the year up into 4 sections can be a straightforward and helpful way to check in on your goals and whether or not you are on task to achieving them. Use this 90 day section to break down your yearly vision into more manageable chunks. Document this carefully and specifically taking care to ensure you're working with achievable targets. You may only have one target for each of the **HOME** sections or you may have lots, both are okay. This process is as unique as families are and this book is here to serve you, so I encourage you to use it in a way that makes sense for your family.

WEEKLY PLAN

Finally, there is a section for specific and trackable weekly plans - 52 of these. This section is for your bite sized targets or plans. Keep these one step ahead of where you are currently at. This section is really exciting as you can see how you are progressing easily. It is in this section that you will be mapping out your strategy and resources required to achieve your vision.

Another useful aspect to this section, is that if you have a bad week and drop some balls, it's okay - you can start afresh next week, nothing lost.

It is vital that you don't feel down on yourself for any weeks missed. Not only is life busy and often stressful, but establishing new habits is never an easy feat. It takes time and sometimes repeated attempts before you are confident in *practicing* your new habits.

My Family/Household Strengths

Each unique family has areas in which they excel! Imagine those families you know of and think, "I wish we were more like that"... However the truth is that each family has amazing strengths and positive attributes. You might be the family that laughs a lot, or communicates well. Maybe you always work well as a team or have a natural compassion for each other. You may want to continue revisiting this page over the year as more and more strengths come to light as you focus on intentionally building connection and legacy making habits.

So, what do you do really well? Think about this one - every family has their strengths and areas in which they excel. What are some of yours?

What are some ways you connect? How do you enjoy each other? What do you love about being together?

What are some of the key mottos or slogans that represent your family? Or the way you approach life together?

What are some things that you feel proud of?

What do you love about your spouse or partner?

What do you love about each of your children? List each one separately.

The Family Legacy Journal

Core Fears...yes, we do need to talk about it

This is a really important subject. Why you ask? Because whether we want it or not, our core fears or anxieties often govern our choices and actions (and we don't even realise it).

These could be fears from childhood about not being a good parent, or fears relating to ongoing family situations in which you feel out of control. Perhaps you struggled with mental health as a teen, perhaps your parents always fought, perhaps you grew up without a father or mother's example as a role model.

For some of us, there are few anxieties or fears. For others there are many. This section is not intended to get you bogged down in the past, but rather to shed some light on areas that will require more deliberation and thought as you move forward.

This section may take some time to complete, and that's okay! But please give it a chance, look over these questions and think about how the answers may be impacting on your family legacy so far. And how you can face these and create the legacy you want for your family from this day forth. This is YOUR family and this is YOUR chance to make it what you want it to be.

When you think of the word "family," what comes to mind?

What kind of parent do you think you are? Your partner is?

What do you not want to repeat from your own experience of growing up?

How does this affect your parenting/relationship?

What is some of the negative self-talk you use about yourself as a parent?

What are some of the things you do not feel ready for as a parent?

Core Visions: H/O/M/E

H - Head and Heart

What are your visions for your spiritual, mental and emotional development?

Are there books you want to read, spiritual practices you want to build as habits or postures of the mind you wish to adopt? What are the daily affirmations you want to use and believe?

ANNUAL VISION

(Blue Sky Goal)

_____

_____

_____

_____

_____

_____

_____

_____

90 DAY VISION

PLAN IT

What resources do you need to acquire/use/source to achieve this goal?

What are the potential blockages to achieving this goal? What do you need to be aware of, look out for and prepare to manage?

How will you know you have achieved this goal? What will it look like? Feel like?

REFLECTION

Did you achieve your vision? If not, what got in the way - how can you reassess and try again? Do you need to pivot and shift your goal post? Or do you need to source/use resources more effectively? Do not be discouraged! Change takes time and is often hard, but is so worth it!

90 DAY VISION

PLAN IT

What resources do you need to acquire/use/source to achieve this goal?

What are the potential blockages to achieving this goal? What do you need to be aware of, look out for and prepare to manage?

How will you know you have achieved this goal? What will it look like? Feel like?

REFLECTION

Did you achieve your vision? If not, what got in the way - how can you reassess and try again? Do you need to pivot and shift your goal post? Or do you need to source/use resources more effectively? Do not be discouraged! Change takes time and is often hard, but is so worth it!

90. DAY VISION

PLAN IT

What resources do you need to acquire/use/source to achieve this goal?

What are the potential blockages to achieving this goal? What do you need to be aware of, look out for and prepare to manage?

How will you know you have achieved this goal? What will it look like? Feel like?

REFLECTION

Did you achieve your vision? If not, what got in the way - how can you reassess and try again? Do you need to pivot and shift your goal post? Or do you need to source/use resources more effectively? Do not be discouraged! Change takes time and is often hard, but is so worth it!

90 DAY VISION

PLAN IT

What resources do you need to acquire/use/source to achieve this goal?

What are the potential blockages to achieving this goal? What do you need to be aware of, look out for and prepare to manage?

How will you know you have achieved this goal? What will it look like? Feel like?

REFLECTION

Did you achieve your vision? If not, what got in the way - how can you reassess and try again? Do you need to pivot and shift your goal post? Or do you need to source/use resources more effectively? Do not be discouraged! Change takes time and is often hard, but is so worth it!

WEEKLY TARGET

Date......................

(Document the "bite sized" pieces of your goal, keep it simple and achievable)

_____

_____

_____

_____

Have you engaged with/organised the resources needed? What are they?

_____

_____

_____

_____

REFLECTION

Notes on what worked well and if you hit your target. What do you need to reassess for next week and try again?

_____

_____

_____

_____

WEEKLY TARGET

Date………………..

(Document the "bite sized" pieces of your goal, keep it simple and achievable)

Have you engaged with/organised the resources needed? What are they?

REFLECTION

Notes on what worked well and if you hit your target. What do you need to reassess for next week and try again?

WEEKLY TARGET

Date………………..

(Document the "bite sized" pieces of your goal, keep it simple and achievable)

_____

_____

_____

Have you engaged with/organised the resources needed? What are they?

_____

_____

_____

REFLECTION

Notes on what worked well and if you hit your target. What do you need to reassess for next week and try again?

_____

_____

_____

WEEKLY TARGET

Date……………..

(Document the "bite sized" pieces of your goal, keep it simple and achievable)

_____

_____

_____

_____

Have you engaged with/organised the resources needed? What are they?

_____

_____

_____

_____

REFLECTION

Notes on what worked well and if you hit your target. What do you need to reassess for next week and try again?

_____

_____

_____

_____

WEEKLY TARGET

Date……………..

(Document the "bite sized" pieces of your goal, keep it simple and achievable)

Have you engaged with/organised the resources needed? What are they?

REFLECTION

Notes on what worked well and if you hit your target. What do you need to reassess for next week and try again?

WEEKLY TARGET

Date……………..

(Document the "bite sized" pieces of your goal, keep it simple and achievable)

_____
_____
_____
_____

Have you engaged with/organised the resources needed? What are they?

_____
_____
_____
_____

REFLECTION

Notes on what worked well and if you hit your target. What do you need to reassess for next week and try again?

_____
_____
_____

WEEKLY TARGET

Date……………..

(Document the "bite sized" pieces of your goal, keep it simple and achievable)

Have you engaged with/organised the resources needed? What are they?

REFLECTION

Notes on what worked well and if you hit your target. What do you need to reassess for next week and try again?

WEEKLY TARGET

Date……………..

(Document the "bite sized" pieces of your goal, keep it simple and achievable)

_____

_____

_____

Have you engaged with/organised the resources needed? What are they?

_____

_____

_____

REFLECTION

Notes on what worked well and if you hit your target. What do you need to reassess for next week and try again?

_____

_____

_____

WEEKLY TARGET

Date..................

(Document the "bite sized" pieces of your goal, keep it simple and achievable)

_____

_____

_____

Have you engaged with/organised the resources needed? What are they?

_____

_____

_____

REFLECTION

Notes on what worked well and if you hit your target. What do you need to reassess for next week and try again?

_____

_____

_____

WEEKLY TARGET

Date...................

(Document the "bite sized" pieces of your goal, keep it simple and achievable)

Have you engaged with/organised the resources needed? What are they?

REFLECTION

Notes on what worked well and if you hit your target. What do you need to reassess for next week and try again?

WEEKLY TARGET

Date..................

(Document the "bite sized" pieces of your goal, keep it simple and achievable)

_____

_____

_____

_____

Have you engaged with/organised the resources needed? What are they?

_____

_____

_____

_____

REFLECTION

Notes on what worked well and if you hit your target. What do you need to reassess for next week and try again?

_____

_____

_____

WEEKLY TARGET

Date....................

(Document the "bite sized" pieces of your goal, keep it simple and achievable)

_____

_____

_____

_____

Have you engaged with/organised the resources needed? What are they?

_____

_____

_____

_____

REFLECTION

Notes on what worked well and if you hit your target. What do you need to reassess for next week and try again?

_____

_____

_____

_____

WEEKLY TARGET

Date……………..

(Document the "bite sized" pieces of your goal, keep it simple and achievable)

_____

_____

_____

_____

Have you engaged with/organised the resources needed? What are they?

_____

_____

_____

_____

REFLECTION

Notes on what worked well and if you hit your target. What do you need to reassess for next week and try again?

_____

_____

_____

WEEKLY TARGET

Date................

(Document the "bite sized" pieces of your goal, keep it simple and achievable)

Have you engaged with/organised the resources needed? What are they?

REFLECTION

Notes on what worked well and if you hit your target. What do you need to reassess for next week and try again?

WEEKLY TARGET

Date.................

(Document the "bite sized" pieces of your goal, keep it simple and achievable)

Have you engaged with/organised the resources needed? What are they?

REFLECTION

Notes on what worked well and if you hit your target. What do you need to reassess for next week and try again?

WEEKLY TARGET

Date………………..

(Document the "bite sized" pieces of your goal, keep it simple and achievable)

_____

_____

_____

_____

Have you engaged with/organised the resources needed? What are they?

_____

_____

_____

_____

REFLECTION

Notes on what worked well and if you hit your target. What do you need to reassess for next week and try again?

_____

_____

_____

WEEKLY TARGET

Date..................

(Document the "bite sized" pieces of your goal, keep it simple and achievable)

_____

_____

_____

_____

Have you engaged with/organised the resources needed? What are they?

_____

_____

_____

_____

REFLECTION

Notes on what worked well and if you hit your target. What do you need to reassess for next week and try again?

_____

_____

_____

_____

WEEKLY TARGET

Date……………..

(Document the "bite sized" pieces of your goal, keep it simple and achievable)

_____

_____

_____

Have you engaged with/organised the resources needed? What are they?

_____

_____

_____

REFLECTION

Notes on what worked well and if you hit your target. What do you need to reassess for next week and try again?

_____

_____

_____

WEEKLY TARGET

Date……………..

(Document the "bite sized" pieces of your goal, keep it simple and achievable)

_____

_____

_____

Have you engaged with/organised the resources needed? What are they?

_____

_____

_____

REFLECTION

Notes on what worked well and if you hit your target. What do you need to reassess for next week and try again?

_____

_____

_____

The Family Legacy Journal

WEEKLY TARGET

Date………………..

(Document the "bite sized" pieces of your goal, keep it simple and achievable)

_____

_____

_____

Have you engaged with/organised the resources needed? What are they?

_____

_____

_____

REFLECTION

Notes on what worked well and if you hit your target. What do you need to reassess for next week and try again?

_____

_____

_____

WEEKLY TARGET

Date……………...

(Document the "bite sized" pieces of your goal, keep it simple and achievable)

Have you engaged with/organised the resources needed? What are they?

REFLECTION

Notes on what worked well and if you hit your target. What do you need to reassess for next week and try again?

WEEKLY TARGET

Date....................

(Document the "bite sized" pieces of your goal, keep it simple and achievable)

_____

_____

_____

_____

Have you engaged with/organised the resources needed? What are they?

_____

_____

_____

_____

REFLECTION

Notes on what worked well and if you hit your target. What do you need to reassess for next week and try again?

_____

_____

_____

The Family Legacy Journal

WEEKLY TARGET

Date………………..

(Document the "bite sized" pieces of your goal, keep it simple and achievable)

_____

_____

_____

Have you engaged with/organised the resources needed? What are they?

_____

_____

_____

REFLECTION

Notes on what worked well and if you hit your target. What do you need to reassess for next week and try again?

_____

_____

_____

WEEKLY TARGET

Date……………..

(Document the "bite sized" pieces of your goal, keep it simple and achievable)

Have you engaged with/organised the resources needed? What are they?

REFLECTION

Notes on what worked well and if you hit your target. What do you need to reassess for next week and try again?

WEEKLY TARGET

Date……………..

(Document the "bite sized" pieces of your goal, keep it simple and achievable)

_____

_____

_____

Have you engaged with/organised the resources needed? What are they?

_____

_____

_____

REFLECTION

Notes on what worked well and if you hit your target. What do you need to reassess for next week and try again?

_____

_____

_____

WEEKLY TARGET

Date……………….

(Document the "bite sized" pieces of your goal, keep it simple and achievable)

_____
_____
_____
_____

Have you engaged with/organised the resources needed? What are they?

_____
_____
_____
_____

REFLECTION

Notes on what worked well and if you hit your target. What do you need to reassess for next week and try again?

_____
_____
_____
_____

The Family Legacy Journal

WEEKLY TARGET

Date………………..

(Document the "bite sized" pieces of your goal, keep it simple and achievable)

Have you engaged with/organised the resources needed? What are they?

REFLECTION

Notes on what worked well and if you hit your target. What do you need to reassess for next week and try again?

WEEKLY TARGET

Date..................

(Document the "bite sized" pieces of your goal, keep it simple and achievable)

_____
_____
_____
_____

Have you engaged with/organised the resources needed? What are they?

_____
_____
_____

REFLECTION

Notes on what worked well and if you hit your target. What do you need to reassess for next week and try again?

_____
_____
_____

WEEKLY TARGET

Date..................

(Document the "bite sized" pieces of your goal, keep it simple and achievable)

_____
_____
_____
_____

Have you engaged with/organised the resources needed? What are they?

_____
_____
_____
_____

REFLECTION

Notes on what worked well and if you hit your target. What do you need to reassess for next week and try again?

_____
_____
_____
_____

WEEKLY TARGET

Date................

(Document the "bite sized" pieces of your goal, keep it simple and achievable)

Have you engaged with/organised the resources needed? What are they?

REFLECTION

Notes on what worked well and if you hit your target. What do you need to reassess for next week and try again?

WEEKLY TARGET

Date..................

(Document the "bite sized" pieces of your goal, keep it simple and achievable)

_____

_____

_____

Have you engaged with/organised the resources needed? What are they?

_____

_____

_____

REFLECTION

Notes on what worked well and if you hit your target. What do you need to reassess for next week and try again?

_____

_____

_____

WEEKLY TARGET

Date………………..

(Document the "bite sized" pieces of your goal, keep it simple and achievable)

Have you engaged with/organised the resources needed? What are they?

REFLECTION

Notes on what worked well and if you hit your target. What do you need to reassess for next week and try again?

WEEKLY TARGET

Date..................

(Document the "bite sized" pieces of your goal, keep it simple and achievable)

_____

_____

_____

Have you engaged with/organised the resources needed? What are they?

_____

_____

_____

REFLECTION

Notes on what worked well and if you hit your target. What do you need to reassess for next week and try again?

_____

_____

_____

WEEKLY TARGET

Date....................

(Document the "bite sized" pieces of your goal, keep it simple and achievable)

Have you engaged with/organised the resources needed? What are they?

REFLECTION

Notes on what worked well and if you hit your target. What do you need to reassess for next week and try again?

WEEKLY TARGET

Date.................

(Document the "bite sized" pieces of your goal, keep it simple and achievable)

_____

_____

_____

_____

Have you engaged with/organised the resources needed? What are they?

_____

_____

_____

_____

REFLECTION

Notes on what worked well and if you hit your target. What do you need to reassess for next week and try again?

_____

_____

_____

_____

WEEKLY TARGET

Date................

(Document the "bite sized" pieces of your goal, keep it simple and achievable)

Have you engaged with/organised the resources needed? What are they?

REFLECTION

Notes on what worked well and if you hit your target. What do you need to reassess for next week and try again?

WEEKLY TARGET

Date………………..

(Document the "bite sized" pieces of your goal, keep it simple and achievable)

_____

_____

_____

Have you engaged with/organised the resources needed? What are they?

_____

_____

_____

REFLECTION

Notes on what worked well and if you hit your target. What do you need to reassess for next week and try again?

_____

_____

_____

WEEKLY TARGET

Date..................

(Document the "bite sized" pieces of your goal, keep it simple and achievable)

_____

_____

_____

_____

Have you engaged with/organised the resources needed? What are they?

_____

_____

_____

_____

REFLECTION

Notes on what worked well and if you hit your target. What do you need to reassess for next week and try again?

_____

_____

_____

_____

WEEKLY TARGET

Date..................

(Document the "bite sized" pieces of your goal, keep it simple and achievable)

_____

_____

_____

Have you engaged with/organised the resources needed? What are they?

_____

_____

_____

REFLECTION

Notes on what worked well and if you hit your target. What do you need to reassess for next week and try again?

_____

_____

_____

WEEKLY TARGET

Date................

(Document the "bite sized" pieces of your goal, keep it simple and achievable)

Have you engaged with/organised the resources needed? What are they?

REFLECTION

Notes on what worked well and if you hit your target. What do you need to reassess for next week and try again?

WEEKLY TARGET

Date………………..

(Document the "bite sized" pieces of your goal, keep it simple and achievable)

_____

_____

_____

Have you engaged with/organised the resources needed? What are they?

_____

_____

_____

REFLECTION

Notes on what worked well and if you hit your target. What do you need to reassess for next week and try again?

_____

_____

_____

WEEKLY TARGET

Date……………..

(Document the "bite sized" pieces of your goal, keep it simple and achievable)

Have you engaged with/organised the resources needed? What are they?

REFLECTION

Notes on what worked well and if you hit your target. What do you need to reassess for next week and try again?

WEEKLY TARGET

Date……………..

(Document the "bite sized" pieces of your goal, keep it simple and achievable)

_____
_____
_____
_____

Have you engaged with/organised the resources needed? What are they?

_____
_____
_____
_____

REFLECTION

Notes on what worked well and if you hit your target. What do you need to reassess for next week and try again?

_____
_____
_____

WEEKLY TARGET

Date………………..

(Document the "bite sized" pieces of your goal, keep it simple and achievable)

Have you engaged with/organised the resources needed? What are they?

REFLECTION

Notes on what worked well and if you hit your target. What do you need to reassess for next week and try again?

The Family Legacy Journal

WEEKLY TARGET

Date………………..

(Document the "bite sized" pieces of your goal, keep it simple and achievable)

_____

_____

_____

Have you engaged with/organised the resources needed? What are they?

_____

_____

_____

REFLECTION

Notes on what worked well and if you hit your target. What do you need to reassess for next week and try again?

_____

_____

_____

WEEKLY TARGET

Date................

(Document the "bite sized" pieces of your goal, keep it simple and achievable)

Have you engaged with/organised the resources needed? What are they?

REFLECTION

Notes on what worked well and if you hit your target. What do you need to reassess for next week and try again?

WEEKLY TARGET

Date………………..

(Document the "bite sized" pieces of your goal, keep it simple and achievable)

_____

_____

_____

Have you engaged with/organised the resources needed? What are they?

_____

_____

_____

REFLECTION

Notes on what worked well and if you hit your target. What do you need to reassess for next week and try again?

_____

_____

_____

WEEKLY TARGET

Date................

(Document the "bite sized" pieces of your goal, keep it simple and achievable)

....

....

....

....

Have you engaged with/organised the resources needed? What are they?

....

....

....

....

REFLECTION

Notes on what worked well and if you hit your target. What do you need to reassess for next week and try again?

....

....

....

WEEKLY TARGET

Date………………..

(Document the "bite sized" pieces of your goal, keep it simple and achievable)

Have you engaged with/organised the resources needed? What are they?

REFLECTION

Notes on what worked well and if you hit your target. What do you need to reassess for next week and try again?

WEEKLY TARGET

Date..................

(Document the "bite sized" pieces of your goal, keep it simple and achievable)

_____

_____

_____

_____

Have you engaged with/organised the resources needed? What are they?

_____

_____

_____

_____

REFLECTION

Notes on what worked well and if you hit your target. What do you need to reassess for next week and try again?

_____

_____

_____

_____

WEEKLY TARGET

Date……………...

(Document the "bite sized" pieces of your goal, keep it simple and achievable)

Have you engaged with/organised the resources needed? What are they?

REFLECTION

Notes on what worked well and if you hit your target. What do you need to reassess for next week and try again?

WEEKLY TARGET

Date……………..

(Document the "bite sized" pieces of your goal, keep it simple and achievable)

Have you engaged with/organised the resources needed? What are they?

REFLECTION

Notes on what worked well and if you hit your target. What do you need to reassess for next week and try again?

O - Others

What is your vision for your relationships?

Choose to set targets relating to your spouse, partner, children, extended family, friends and community? Keep it achievable and realistic, relationships are complex and sometimes it can be best to start simple and over time go deeper. Remember to consider all things about culture, habits, traditions and connection.

ANNUAL VISION

(Blue Sky Goal)

_____
_____
_____
_____
_____
_____
_____
_____

90 DAY VISION

PLAN IT

What resources do you need to acquire/use/source to achieve this goal?

What are the potential blockages to achieving this goal? What do you need to be aware of, look out for and prepare to manage?

How will you know you have achieved this goal? What will it look like? Feel like?

REFLECTION

Did you achieve your vision? If not, what got in the way - how can you reassess and try again? Do you need to pivot and shift your goal post? Or do you need to source/use resources more effectively? Do not be discouraged! Change takes time and is often hard, but is so worth it!

90 DAY VISION

PLAN IT

What resources do you need to acquire/use/source to achieve this goal?

What are the potential blockages to achieving this goal? What do you need to be aware of, look out for and prepare to manage?

How will you know you have achieved this goal? What will it look like? Feel like?

REFLECTION

Did you achieve your vision? If not, what got in the way - how can you reassess and try again? Do you need to pivot and shift your goal post? Or do you need to source/use resources more effectively? Do not be discouraged! Change takes time and is often hard, but is so worth it!

90 DAY VISION

PLAN IT

What resources do you need to acquire/use/source to achieve this goal?

What are the potential blockages to achieving this goal? What do you need to be aware of, look out for and prepare to manage?

How will you know you have achieved this goal? What will it look like? Feel like?

REFLECTION

Did you achieve your vision? If not, what got in the way - how can you reassess and try again? Do you need to pivot and shift your goal post? Or do you need to source/use resources more effectively? Do not be discouraged! Change takes time and is often hard, but is so worth it!

90 DAY VISION

PLAN IT

What resources do you need to acquire/use/source to achieve this goal?

What are the potential blockages to achieving this goal? What do you need to be aware of, look out for and prepare to manage?

How will you know you have achieved this goal? What will it look like? Feel like?

REFLECTION

Did you achieve your vision? If not, what got in the way - how can you reassess and try again? Do you need to pivot and shift your goal post? Or do you need to source/use resources more effectively? Do not be discouraged! Change takes time and is often hard, but is so worth it!

WEEKLY TARGET

Date.................

(Document the "bite sized" pieces of your goal, keep it simple and achievable)

Have you engaged with/organised the resources needed? What are they?

REFLECTION

Notes on what worked well and if you hit your target. What do you need to reassess for next week and try again?

WEEKLY TARGET

Date.................

(Document the "bite sized" pieces of your goal, keep it simple and achievable)

Have you engaged with/organised the resources needed? What are they?

REFLECTION

Notes on what worked well and if you hit your target. What do you need to reassess for next week and try again?

WEEKLY TARGET

Date……………..

(Document the "bite sized" pieces of your goal, keep it simple and achievable)

Have you engaged with/organised the resources needed? What are they?

REFLECTION

Notes on what worked well and if you hit your target. What do you need to reassess for next week and try again?

WEEKLY TARGET

Date……………..

(Document the "bite sized" pieces of your goal, keep it simple and achievable)

Have you engaged with/organised the resources needed? What are they?

REFLECTION

Notes on what worked well and if you hit your target. What do you need to reassess for next week and try again?

WEEKLY TARGET

Date……………..

(Document the "bite sized" pieces of your goal, keep it simple and achievable)

Have you engaged with/organised the resources needed? What are they?

REFLECTION

Notes on what worked well and if you hit your target. What do you need to reassess for next week and try again?

WEEKLY TARGET

Date................

(Document the "bite sized" pieces of your goal, keep it simple and achievable)

Have you engaged with/organised the resources needed? What are they?

REFLECTION

Notes on what worked well and if you hit your target. What do you need to reassess for next week and try again?

WEEKLY TARGET

Date……………..

(Document the "bite sized" pieces of your goal, keep it simple and achievable)

_____
_____
_____
_____

Have you engaged with/organised the resources needed? What are they?

_____
_____
_____
_____

REFLECTION

Notes on what worked well and if you hit your target. What do you need to reassess for next week and try again?

_____
_____
_____

WEEKLY TARGET

Date……………..

(Document the "bite sized" pieces of your goal, keep it simple and achievable)

Have you engaged with/organised the resources needed? What are they?

REFLECTION

Notes on what worked well and if you hit your target. What do you need to reassess for next week and try again?

WEEKLY TARGET

Date……………..

(Document the "bite sized" pieces of your goal, keep it simple and achievable)

Have you engaged with/organised the resources needed? What are they?

REFLECTION

Notes on what worked well and if you hit your target. What do you need to reassess for next week and try again?

WEEKLY TARGET

Date……………..

(Document the "bite sized" pieces of your goal, keep it simple and achievable)

_____
_____
_____

Have you engaged with/organised the resources needed? What are they?

_____
_____
_____

REFLECTION

Notes on what worked well and if you hit your target. What do you need to reassess for next week and try again?

_____
_____
_____

WEEKLY TARGET

Date……………..

(Document the "bite sized" pieces of your goal, keep it simple and achievable)

Have you engaged with/organised the resources needed? What are they?

REFLECTION

Notes on what worked well and if you hit your target. What do you need to reassess for next week and try again?

WEEKLY TARGET

Date………………..

(Document the "bite sized" pieces of your goal, keep it simple and achievable)

_____

_____

_____

_____

Have you engaged with/organised the resources needed? What are they?

_____

_____

_____

_____

REFLECTION

Notes on what worked well and if you hit your target. What do you need to reassess for next week and try again?

_____

_____

_____

_____

WEEKLY TARGET

Date....................

(Document the "bite sized" pieces of your goal, keep it simple and achievable)

Have you engaged with/organised the resources needed? What are they?

REFLECTION

Notes on what worked well and if you hit your target. What do you need to reassess for next week and try again?

WEEKLY TARGET

Date.................

(Document the "bite sized" pieces of your goal, keep it simple and achievable)

Have you engaged with/organised the resources needed? What are they?

REFLECTION

Notes on what worked well and if you hit your target. What do you need to reassess for next week and try again?

WEEKLY TARGET

Date……………..

(Document the "bite sized" pieces of your goal, keep it simple and achievable)

_____

_____

_____

_____

Have you engaged with/organised the resources needed? What are they?

_____

_____

_____

_____

REFLECTION

Notes on what worked well and if you hit your target. What do you need to reassess for next week and try again?

_____

_____

_____

WEEKLY TARGET

Date...................

(Document the "bite sized" pieces of your goal, keep it simple and achievable)

Have you engaged with/organised the resources needed? What are they?

REFLECTION

Notes on what worked well and if you hit your target. What do you need to reassess for next week and try again?

WEEKLY TARGET

Date.....................

(Document the "bite sized" pieces of your goal, keep it simple and achievable)

_____

_____

_____

_____

Have you engaged with/organised the resources needed? What are they?

_____

_____

_____

_____

REFLECTION

Notes on what worked well and if you hit your target. What do you need to reassess for next week and try again?

_____

_____

WEEKLY TARGET

Date……………..

(Document the "bite sized" pieces of your goal, keep it simple and achievable)

_____

_____

_____

Have you engaged with/organised the resources needed? What are they?

_____

_____

_____

REFLECTION

Notes on what worked well and if you hit your target. What do you need to reassess for next week and try again?

_____

_____

_____

WEEKLY TARGET

Date..................

(Document the "bite sized" pieces of your goal, keep it simple and achievable)

_____

_____

_____

_____

Have you engaged with/organised the resources needed? What are they?

_____

_____

_____

_____

REFLECTION

Notes on what worked well and if you hit your target. What do you need to reassess for next week and try again?

_____

_____

WEEKLY TARGET

Date..................

(Document the "bite sized" pieces of your goal, keep it simple and achievable)

_____

_____

_____

_____

Have you engaged with/organised the resources needed? What are they?

_____

_____

_____

_____

REFLECTION

Notes on what worked well and if you hit your target. What do you need to reassess for next week and try again?

_____

_____

_____

_____

WEEKLY TARGET

Date………………..

(Document the "bite sized" pieces of your goal, keep it simple and achievable)

_____

_____

_____

_____

Have you engaged with/organised the resources needed? What are they?

_____

_____

_____

_____

REFLECTION

Notes on what worked well and if you hit your target. What do you need to reassess for next week and try again?

_____

_____

_____

WEEKLY TARGET

Date.................

(Document the "bite sized" pieces of your goal, keep it simple and achievable)

_____

_____

_____

_____

Have you engaged with/organised the resources needed? What are they?

_____

_____

_____

_____

REFLECTION

Notes on what worked well and if you hit your target. What do you need to reassess for next week and try again?

_____

_____

_____

_____

WEEKLY TARGET

Date……………..

(Document the "bite sized" pieces of your goal, keep it simple and achievable)

Have you engaged with/organised the resources needed? What are they?

REFLECTION

Notes on what worked well and if you hit your target. What do you need to reassess for next week and try again?

WEEKLY TARGET

Date……………..

(Document the "bite sized" pieces of your goal, keep it simple and achievable)

Have you engaged with/organised the resources needed? What are they?

REFLECTION

Notes on what worked well and if you hit your target. What do you need to reassess for next week and try again?

WEEKLY TARGET

Date....................

(Document the "bite sized" pieces of your goal, keep it simple and achievable)

Have you engaged with/organised the resources needed? What are they?

REFLECTION

Notes on what worked well and if you hit your target. What do you need to reassess for next week and try again?

WEEKLY TARGET

Date……………..

(Document the "bite sized" pieces of your goal, keep it simple and achievable)

_____

_____

_____

_____

Have you engaged with/organised the resources needed? What are they?

_____

_____

_____

_____

REFLECTION

Notes on what worked well and if you hit your target. What do you need to reassess for next week and try again?

_____

_____

_____

_____

WEEKLY TARGET

Date..................

(Document the "bite sized" pieces of your goal, keep it simple and achievable)

_____

_____

_____

Have you engaged with/organised the resources needed? What are they?

_____

_____

_____

REFLECTION

Notes on what worked well and if you hit your target. What do you need to reassess for next week and try again?

_____

_____

_____

WEEKLY TARGET

Date.................

(Document the "bite sized" pieces of your goal, keep it simple and achievable)

_____

_____

_____

_____

Have you engaged with/organised the resources needed? What are they?

_____

_____

_____

_____

REFLECTION

Notes on what worked well and if you hit your target. What do you need to reassess for next week and try again?

_____

_____

_____

_____

WEEKLY TARGET

Date................

(Document the "bite sized" pieces of your goal, keep it simple and achievable)

Have you engaged with/organised the resources needed? What are they?

REFLECTION

Notes on what worked well and if you hit your target. What do you need to reassess for next week and try again?

WEEKLY TARGET

Date..................

(Document the "bite sized" pieces of your goal, keep it simple and achievable)

_____

_____

_____

Have you engaged with/organised the resources needed? What are they?

_____

_____

_____

REFLECTION

Notes on what worked well and if you hit your target. What do you need to reassess for next week and try again?

_____

_____

_____

WEEKLY TARGET

Date...................

(Document the "bite sized" pieces of your goal, keep it simple and achievable)

Have you engaged with/organised the resources needed? What are they?

REFLECTION

Notes on what worked well and if you hit your target. What do you need to reassess for next week and try again?

WEEKLY TARGET

Date.................

(Document the "bite sized" pieces of your goal, keep it simple and achievable)

Have you engaged with/organised the resources needed? What are they?

REFLECTION

Notes on what worked well and if you hit your target. What do you need to reassess for next week and try again?

WEEKLY TARGET

Date..................

(Document the "bite sized" pieces of your goal, keep it simple and achievable)

Have you engaged with/organised the resources needed? What are they?

REFLECTION

Notes on what worked well and if you hit your target. What do you need to reassess for next week and try again?

WEEKLY TARGET

Date....................

(Document the "bite sized" pieces of your goal, keep it simple and achievable)

Have you engaged with/organised the resources needed? What are they?

REFLECTION

Notes on what worked well and if you hit your target. What do you need to reassess for next week and try again?

WEEKLY TARGET

Date……………..

(Document the "bite sized" pieces of your goal, keep it simple and achievable)

Have you engaged with/organised the resources needed? What are they?

REFLECTION

Notes on what worked well and if you hit your target. What do you need to reassess for next week and try again?

WEEKLY TARGET

Date...................

(Document the "bite sized" pieces of your goal, keep it simple and achievable)

Have you engaged with/organised the resources needed? What are they?

REFLECTION

Notes on what worked well and if you hit your target. What do you need to reassess for next week and try again?

WEEKLY TARGET

Date……………..

(Document the "bite sized" pieces of your goal, keep it simple and achievable)

Have you engaged with/organised the resources needed? What are they?

REFLECTION

Notes on what worked well and if you hit your target. What do you need to reassess for next week and try again?

WEEKLY TARGET

Date……………..

(Document the "bite sized" pieces of your goal, keep it simple and achievable)

Have you engaged with/organised the resources needed? What are they?

REFLECTION

Notes on what worked well and if you hit your target. What do you need to reassess for next week and try again?

WEEKLY TARGET

Date................

(Document the "bite sized" pieces of your goal, keep it simple and achievable)

Have you engaged with/organised the resources needed? What are they?

REFLECTION

Notes on what worked well and if you hit your target. What do you need to reassess for next week and try again?

WEEKLY TARGET

Date.................

(Document the "bite sized" pieces of your goal, keep it simple and achievable)

Have you engaged with/organised the resources needed? What are they?

REFLECTION

Notes on what worked well and if you hit your target. What do you need to reassess for next week and try again?

WEEKLY TARGET

Date……………..

(Document the "bite sized" pieces of your goal, keep it simple and achievable)

_____

_____

_____

_____

Have you engaged with/organised the resources needed? What are they?

_____

_____

_____

_____

REFLECTION

Notes on what worked well and if you hit your target. What do you need to reassess for next week and try again?

_____

_____

_____

WEEKLY TARGET

Date……………..

(Document the "bite sized" pieces of your goal, keep it simple and achievable)

Have you engaged with/organised the resources needed? What are they?

REFLECTION

Notes on what worked well and if you hit your target. What do you need to reassess for next week and try again?

WEEKLY TARGET

Date................

(Document the "bite sized" pieces of your goal, keep it simple and achievable)

_____
_____
_____

Have you engaged with/organised the resources needed? What are they?

_____
_____
_____

REFLECTION

Notes on what worked well and if you hit your target. What do you need to reassess for next week and try again?

_____
_____
_____

WEEKLY TARGET

Date...................

(Document the "bite sized" pieces of your goal, keep it simple and achievable)

Have you engaged with/organised the resources needed? What are they?

REFLECTION

Notes on what worked well and if you hit your target. What do you need to reassess for next week and try again?

WEEKLY TARGET

Date………………..

(Document the "bite sized" pieces of your goal, keep it simple and achievable)

_____
_____
_____
_____

Have you engaged with/organised the resources needed? What are they?

_____
_____
_____
_____

REFLECTION

Notes on what worked well and if you hit your target. What do you need to reassess for next week and try again?

_____
_____
_____

WEEKLY TARGET

Date………………..

(Document the "bite sized" pieces of your goal, keep it simple and achievable)

Have you engaged with/organised the resources needed? What are they?

REFLECTION

Notes on what worked well and if you hit your target. What do you need to reassess for next week and try again?

WEEKLY TARGET

Date……………..

(Document the "bite sized" pieces of your goal, keep it simple and achievable)

Have you engaged with/organised the resources needed? What are they?

REFLECTION

Notes on what worked well and if you hit your target. What do you need to reassess for next week and try again?

WEEKLY TARGET

Date................

(Document the "bite sized" pieces of your goal, keep it simple and achievable)

Have you engaged with/organised the resources needed? What are they?

REFLECTION

Notes on what worked well and if you hit your target. What do you need to reassess for next week and try again?

WEEKLY TARGET

Date................

(Document the "bite sized" pieces of your goal, keep it simple and achievable)

_____
_____
_____
_____

Have you engaged with/organised the resources needed? What are they?

_____
_____
_____
_____

REFLECTION

Notes on what worked well and if you hit your target. What do you need to reassess for next week and try again?

_____
_____
_____
_____

WEEKLY TARGET

Date.................

(Document the "bite sized" pieces of your goal, keep it simple and achievable)

⎯⎯⎯⎯⎯⎯⎯⎯⎯⎯⎯⎯⎯⎯⎯⎯⎯⎯⎯⎯⎯⎯⎯⎯⎯⎯⎯⎯⎯⎯⎯⎯⎯⎯⎯⎯⎯⎯

⎯⎯⎯⎯⎯⎯⎯⎯⎯⎯⎯⎯⎯⎯⎯⎯⎯⎯⎯⎯⎯⎯⎯⎯⎯⎯⎯⎯⎯⎯⎯⎯⎯⎯⎯⎯⎯⎯

⎯⎯⎯⎯⎯⎯⎯⎯⎯⎯⎯⎯⎯⎯⎯⎯⎯⎯⎯⎯⎯⎯⎯⎯⎯⎯⎯⎯⎯⎯⎯⎯⎯⎯⎯⎯⎯⎯

Have you engaged with/organised the resources needed? What are they?

⎯⎯⎯⎯⎯⎯⎯⎯⎯⎯⎯⎯⎯⎯⎯⎯⎯⎯⎯⎯⎯⎯⎯⎯⎯⎯⎯⎯⎯⎯⎯⎯⎯⎯⎯⎯⎯⎯

⎯⎯⎯⎯⎯⎯⎯⎯⎯⎯⎯⎯⎯⎯⎯⎯⎯⎯⎯⎯⎯⎯⎯⎯⎯⎯⎯⎯⎯⎯⎯⎯⎯⎯⎯⎯⎯⎯

⎯⎯⎯⎯⎯⎯⎯⎯⎯⎯⎯⎯⎯⎯⎯⎯⎯⎯⎯⎯⎯⎯⎯⎯⎯⎯⎯⎯⎯⎯⎯⎯⎯⎯⎯⎯⎯⎯

REFLECTION

Notes on what worked well and if you hit your target. What do you need to reassess for next week and try again?

⎯⎯⎯⎯⎯⎯⎯⎯⎯⎯⎯⎯⎯⎯⎯⎯⎯⎯⎯⎯⎯⎯⎯⎯⎯⎯⎯⎯⎯⎯⎯⎯⎯⎯⎯⎯⎯⎯

⎯⎯⎯⎯⎯⎯⎯⎯⎯⎯⎯⎯⎯⎯⎯⎯⎯⎯⎯⎯⎯⎯⎯⎯⎯⎯⎯⎯⎯⎯⎯⎯⎯⎯⎯⎯⎯⎯

⎯⎯⎯⎯⎯⎯⎯⎯⎯⎯⎯⎯⎯⎯⎯⎯⎯⎯⎯⎯⎯⎯⎯⎯⎯⎯⎯⎯⎯⎯⎯⎯⎯⎯⎯⎯⎯⎯

WEEKLY TARGET

Date.................

(Document the "bite sized" pieces of your goal, keep it simple and achievable)

_____

_____

_____

Have you engaged with/organised the resources needed? What are they?

_____

_____

_____

REFLECTION

Notes on what worked well and if you hit your target. What do you need to reassess for next week and try again?

_____

_____

_____

WEEKLY TARGET

Date......................

(Document the "bite sized" pieces of your goal, keep it simple and achievable)

_____

_____

_____

Have you engaged with/organised the resources needed? What are they?

_____

_____

_____

REFLECTION

Notes on what worked well and if you hit your target. What do you need to reassess for next week and try again?

_____

_____

_____

M - Movement & Metabolism

What is your vision for your and your family's health? What are the next steps to healthier, happier bodies? What do you need to achieve so that your body is a resource to you? Or what can you do to challenge yourself to the next level of fitness and health?

ANNUAL VISION

(Blue Sky Goal)

The Family Legacy Journal

90 DAY VISION

PLAN IT

What resources do you need to acquire/use/source to achieve this goal?

What are the potential blockages to achieving this goal? What do you need to be aware of, look out for and prepare to manage?

How will you know you have achieved this goal? What will it look like? Feel like?

REFLECTION

Did you achieve your vision? If not, what got in the way - how can you reassess and try again? Do you need to pivot and shift your goal post? Or do you need to source/use resources more effectively? Do not be discouraged! Change takes time and is often hard, but is so worth it!

90 DAY VISION

PLAN IT

What resources do you need to acquire/use/source to achieve this goal?

What are the potential blockages to achieving this goal? What do you need to be aware of, look out for and prepare to manage?

How will you know you have achieved this goal? What will it look like? Feel like?

REFLECTION

Did you achieve your vision? If not, what got in the way - how can you reassess and try again? Do you need to pivot and shift your goal post? Or do you need to source/use resources more effectively? Do not be discouraged! Change takes time and is often hard, but is so worth it!

90 DAY VISION

PLAN IT

What resources do you need to acquire/use/source to achieve this goal?

The Family Legacy Journal

What are the potential blockages to achieving this goal? What do you need to be aware of, look out for and prepare to manage?

How will you know you have achieved this goal? What will it look like? Feel like?

REFLECTION

Did you achieve your vision? If not, what got in the way - how can you reassess and try again? Do you need to pivot and shift your goal post? Or do you need to source/use resources more effectively? Do not be discouraged! Change takes time and is often hard, but is so worth it!

90 DAY VISION

PLAN IT

What resources do you need to acquire/use/source to achieve this goal?

What are the potential blockages to achieving this goal? What do you need to be aware of, look out for and prepare to manage?

How will you know you have achieved this goal? What will it look like? Feel like?

REFLECTION

Did you achieve your vision? If not, what got in the way - how can you reassess and try again? Do you need to pivot and shift your goal post? Or do you need to source/use resources more effectively? Do not be discouraged! Change takes time and is often hard, but is so worth it!

WEEKLY TARGET

Date……………...

(Document the "bite sized" pieces of your goal, keep it simple and achievable)

Have you engaged with/organised the resources needed? What are they?

REFLECTION

Notes on what worked well and if you hit your target. What do you need to reassess for next week and try again?

WEEKLY TARGET

Date……………..

(Document the "bite sized" pieces of your goal, keep it simple and achievable)

Have you engaged with/organised the resources needed? What are they?

REFLECTION

Notes on what worked well and if you hit your target. What do you need to reassess for next week and try again?

WEEKLY TARGET

Date……………..

(Document the "bite sized" pieces of your goal, keep it simple and achievable)

Have you engaged with/organised the resources needed? What are they?

REFLECTION

Notes on what worked well and if you hit your target. What do you need to reassess for next week and try again?

WEEKLY TARGET

Date……………...

(Document the "bite sized" pieces of your goal, keep it simple and achievable)

Have you engaged with/organised the resources needed? What are they?

REFLECTION

Notes on what worked well and if you hit your target. What do you need to reassess for next week and try again?

WEEKLY TARGET

Date..................

(Document the "bite sized" pieces of your goal, keep it simple and achievable)

―――――――――――――――――――――――
―――――――――――――――――――――――
―――――――――――――――――――――――

Have you engaged with/organised the resources needed? What are they?

―――――――――――――――――――――――
―――――――――――――――――――――――
―――――――――――――――――――――――

REFLECTION

Notes on what worked well and if you hit your target. What do you need to reassess for next week and try again?

―――――――――――――――――――――――
―――――――――――――――――――――――
―――――――――――――――――――――――

WEEKLY TARGET

Date……………..

(Document the "bite sized" pieces of your goal, keep it simple and achievable)

Have you engaged with/organised the resources needed? What are they?

REFLECTION

Notes on what worked well and if you hit your target. What do you need to reassess for next week and try again?

WEEKLY TARGET

Date………………..

(Document the "bite sized" pieces of your goal, keep it simple and achievable)

_____

_____

_____

_____

Have you engaged with/organised the resources needed? What are they?

_____

_____

_____

_____

REFLECTION

Notes on what worked well and if you hit your target. What do you need to reassess for next week and try again?

_____

_____

_____

_____

WEEKLY TARGET

Date……………..

(Document the "bite sized" pieces of your goal, keep it simple and achievable)

_____
_____
_____
_____

Have you engaged with/organised the resources needed? What are they?

_____
_____
_____
_____

REFLECTION

Notes on what worked well and if you hit your target. What do you need to reassess for next week and try again?

_____
_____
_____

WEEKLY TARGET

Date................

(Document the "bite sized" pieces of your goal, keep it simple and achievable)

REFLECTION

Have you engaged with/organised the resources needed? What are they?

REFLECTION

Notes on what worked well and if you hit your target. What do you need to reassess for next week and try again?

WEEKLY TARGET

Date……………..

(Document the "bite sized" pieces of your goal, keep it simple and achievable)

_____
_____
_____

Have you engaged with/organised the resources needed? What are they?

_____
_____
_____

REFLECTION

Notes on what worked well and if you hit your target. What do you need to reassess for next week and try again?

_____
_____
_____

WEEKLY TARGET

Date………………..

(Document the "bite sized" pieces of your goal, keep it simple and achievable)

_____
_____
_____

Have you engaged with/organised the resources needed? What are they?

_____
_____
_____

REFLECTION

Notes on what worked well and if you hit your target. What do you need to reassess for next week and try again?

_____
_____
_____

WEEKLY TARGET

Date………………..

(Document the "bite sized" pieces of your goal, keep it simple and achievable)

Have you engaged with/organised the resources needed? What are they?

REFLECTION

Notes on what worked well and if you hit your target. What do you need to reassess for next week and try again?

The Family Legacy Journal

WEEKLY TARGET

Date………………..

(Document the "bite sized" pieces of your goal, keep it simple and achievable)

_____

_____

_____

Have you engaged with/organised the resources needed? What are they?

_____

_____

_____

REFLECTION

Notes on what worked well and if you hit your target. What do you need to reassess for next week and try again?

_____

_____

_____

WEEKLY TARGET

Date..................

(Document the "bite sized" pieces of your goal, keep it simple and achievable)

Have you engaged with/organised the resources needed? What are they?

REFLECTION

Notes on what worked well and if you hit your target. What do you need to reassess for next week and try again?

WEEKLY TARGET

Date..................

(Document the "bite sized" pieces of your goal, keep it simple and achievable)

———————————————————————
———————————————————————
———————————————————————

Have you engaged with/organised the resources needed? What are they?

———————————————————————
———————————————————————
———————————————————————

REFLECTION

Notes on what worked well and if you hit your target. What do you need to reassess for next week and try again?

———————————————————————
———————————————————————

The Family Legacy Journal

WEEKLY TARGET

Date.................

(Document the "bite sized" pieces of your goal, keep it simple and achievable)

———————————————————————
———————————————————————
———————————————————————

Have you engaged with/organised the resources needed? What are they?

———————————————————————
———————————————————————
———————————————————————

REFLECTION

Notes on what worked well and if you hit your target. What do you need to reassess for next week and try again?

———————————————————————
———————————————————————
———————————————————————

WEEKLY TARGET

Date……………..

(Document the "bite sized" pieces of your goal, keep it simple and achievable)

_____

_____

_____

Have you engaged with/organised the resources needed? What are they?

_____

_____

_____

REFLECTION

Notes on what worked well and if you hit your target. What do you need to reassess for next week and try again?

_____

_____

_____

WEEKLY TARGET

Date.................

(Document the "bite sized" pieces of your goal, keep it simple and achievable)

Have you engaged with/organised the resources needed? What are they?

REFLECTION

Notes on what worked well and if you hit your target. What do you need to reassess for next week and try again?

WEEKLY TARGET

Date………………..

(Document the "bite sized" pieces of your goal, keep it simple and achievable)

Have you engaged with/organised the resources needed? What are they?

REFLECTION

Notes on what worked well and if you hit your target. What do you need to reassess for next week and try again?

WEEKLY TARGET

Date……………..

(Document the "bite sized" pieces of your goal, keep it simple and achievable)

Have you engaged with/organised the resources needed? What are they?

REFLECTION

Notes on what worked well and if you hit your target. What do you need to reassess for next week and try again?

WEEKLY TARGET

Date..................

(Document the "bite sized" pieces of your goal, keep it simple and achievable)

Have you engaged with/organised the resources needed? What are they?

REFLECTION

Notes on what worked well and if you hit your target. What do you need to reassess for next week and try again?

The Family Legacy Journal

WEEKLY TARGET

Date……………...

(Document the "bite sized" pieces of your goal, keep it simple and achievable)

_____

_____

_____

Have you engaged with/organised the resources needed? What are they?

_____

_____

_____

REFLECTION

Notes on what worked well and if you hit your target. What do you need to reassess for next week and try again?

_____

_____

_____

WEEKLY TARGET

Date.................

(Document the "bite sized" pieces of your goal, keep it simple and achievable)

Have you engaged with/organised the resources needed? What are they?

REFLECTION

Notes on what worked well and if you hit your target. What do you need to reassess for next week and try again?

WEEKLY TARGET

Date..................

(Document the "bite sized" pieces of your goal, keep it simple and achievable)

_____

_____

_____

Have you engaged with/organised the resources needed? What are they?

_____

_____

_____

REFLECTION

Notes on what worked well and if you hit your target. What do you need to reassess for next week and try again?

_____

_____

_____

WEEKLY TARGET

Date……………..

(Document the "bite sized" pieces of your goal, keep it simple and achievable)

Have you engaged with/organised the resources needed? What are they?

REFLECTION

Notes on what worked well and if you hit your target. What do you need to reassess for next week and try again?

WEEKLY TARGET

Date……………..

(Document the "bite sized" pieces of your goal, keep it simple and achievable)

———————————————————————

———————————————————————

———————————————————————

Have you engaged with/organised the resources needed? What are they?

———————————————————————

———————————————————————

———————————————————————

REFLECTION

Notes on what worked well and if you hit your target. What do you need to reassess for next week and try again?

———————————————————————

———————————————————————

———————————————————————

WEEKLY TARGET

Date……………..

(Document the "bite sized" pieces of your goal, keep it simple and achievable)

Have you engaged with/organised the resources needed? What are they?

REFLECTION

Notes on what worked well and if you hit your target. What do you need to reassess for next week and try again?

WEEKLY TARGET

Date………………..

(Document the "bite sized" pieces of your goal, keep it simple and achievable)

_____
_____
_____

Have you engaged with/organised the resources needed? What are they?

_____
_____
_____

REFLECTION

Notes on what worked well and if you hit your target. What do you need to reassess for next week and try again?

_____
_____
_____

The Family Legacy Journal

WEEKLY TARGET

Date………………..

(Document the "bite sized" pieces of your goal, keep it simple and achievable)

Have you engaged with/organised the resources needed? What are they?

REFLECTION

Notes on what worked well and if you hit your target. What do you need to reassess for next week and try again?

WEEKLY TARGET

Date……………..

(Document the "bite sized" pieces of your goal, keep it simple and achievable)

Have you engaged with/organised the resources needed? What are they?

REFLECTION

Notes on what worked well and if you hit your target. What do you need to reassess for next week and try again?

WEEKLY TARGET

Date……………..

(Document the "bite sized" pieces of your goal, keep it simple and achievable)

Have you engaged with/organised the resources needed? What are they?

REFLECTION

Notes on what worked well and if you hit your target. What do you need to reassess for next week and try again?

WEEKLY TARGET

Date...................

(Document the "bite sized" pieces of your goal, keep it simple and achievable)

Have you engaged with/organised the resources needed? What are they?

REFLECTION

Notes on what worked well and if you hit your target. What do you need to reassess for next week and try again?

WEEKLY TARGET

Date……………..

(Document the "bite sized" pieces of your goal, keep it simple and achievable)

Have you engaged with/organised the resources needed? What are they?

REFLECTION

Notes on what worked well and if you hit your target. What do you need to reassess for next week and try again?

WEEKLY TARGET

Date………………..

(Document the "bite sized" pieces of your goal, keep it simple and achievable)

_____

_____

_____

Have you engaged with/organised the resources needed? What are they?

_____

_____

_____

REFLECTION

Notes on what worked well and if you hit your target. What do you need to reassess for next week and try again?

_____

_____

_____

WEEKLY TARGET

Date...................

(Document the "bite sized" pieces of your goal, keep it simple and achievable)

_____

_____

_____

Have you engaged with/organised the resources needed? What are they?

_____

_____

_____

REFLECTION

Notes on what worked well and if you hit your target. What do you need to reassess for next week and try again?

_____

_____

_____

WEEKLY TARGET

Date……………..

(Document the "bite sized" pieces of your goal, keep it simple and achievable)

Have you engaged with/organised the resources needed? What are they?

REFLECTION

Notes on what worked well and if you hit your target. What do you need to reassess for next week and try again?

WEEKLY TARGET

Date……………..

(Document the "bite sized" pieces of your goal, keep it simple and achievable)

_____

_____

_____

Have you engaged with/organised the resources needed? What are they?

_____

_____

_____

REFLECTION

Notes on what worked well and if you hit your target. What do you need to reassess for next week and try again?

_____

_____

WEEKLY TARGET

Date...................

(Document the "bite sized" pieces of your goal, keep it simple and achievable)

_____

_____

_____

_____

Have you engaged with/organised the resources needed? What are they?

_____

_____

_____

_____

REFLECTION

Notes on what worked well and if you hit your target. What do you need to reassess for next week and try again?

_____

_____

_____

_____

WEEKLY TARGET

Date………………..

(Document the "bite sized" pieces of your goal, keep it simple and achievable)

Have you engaged with/organised the resources needed? What are they?

REFLECTION

Notes on what worked well and if you hit your target. What do you need to reassess for next week and try again?

WEEKLY TARGET

Date……………..

(Document the "bite sized" pieces of your goal, keep it simple and achievable)

_____

_____

_____

_____

Have you engaged with/organised the resources needed? What are they?

_____

_____

_____

_____

REFLECTION

Notes on what worked well and if you hit your target. What do you need to reassess for next week and try again?

_____

_____

_____

WEEKLY TARGET

Date...................

(Document the "bite sized" pieces of your goal, keep it simple and achievable)

_____

_____

_____

Have you engaged with/organised the resources needed? What are they?

_____

_____

_____

REFLECTION

Notes on what worked well and if you hit your target. What do you need to reassess for next week and try again?

_____

_____

_____

WEEKLY TARGET

Date......................

(Document the "bite sized" pieces of your goal, keep it simple and achievable)

Have you engaged with/organised the resources needed? What are they?

REFLECTION

Notes on what worked well and if you hit your target. What do you need to reassess for next week and try again?

WEEKLY TARGET

Date..................

(Document the "bite sized" pieces of your goal, keep it simple and achievable)

Have you engaged with/organised the resources needed? What are they?

REFLECTION

Notes on what worked well and if you hit your target. What do you need to reassess for next week and try again?

The Family Legacy Journal

WEEKLY TARGET

Date………………..

(Document the "bite sized" pieces of your goal, keep it simple and achievable)

_____

_____

_____

_____

Have you engaged with/organised the resources needed? What are they?

_____

_____

_____

_____

REFLECTION

Notes on what worked well and if you hit your target. What do you need to reassess for next week and try again?

_____

_____

_____

_____

WEEKLY TARGET

Date..................

(Document the "bite sized" pieces of your goal, keep it simple and achievable)

Have you engaged with/organised the resources needed? What are they?

REFLECTION

Notes on what worked well and if you hit your target. What do you need to reassess for next week and try again?

WEEKLY TARGET

Date……………...

(Document the "bite sized" pieces of your goal, keep it simple and achievable)

Have you engaged with/organised the resources needed? What are they?

REFLECTION

Notes on what worked well and if you hit your target. What do you need to reassess for next week and try again?

WEEKLY TARGET

Date.................

(Document the "bite sized" pieces of your goal, keep it simple and achievable)

―――――――――――――――――――――――――――
―――――――――――――――――――――――――――
―――――――――――――――――――――――――――

Have you engaged with/organised the resources needed? What are they?

―――――――――――――――――――――――――――
―――――――――――――――――――――――――――
―――――――――――――――――――――――――――

REFLECTION

Notes on what worked well and if you hit your target. What do you need to reassess for next week and try again?

―――――――――――――――――――――――――――
―――――――――――――――――――――――――――
―――――――――――――――――――――――――――

WEEKLY TARGET

Date……………..

(Document the "bite sized" pieces of your goal, keep it simple and achievable)

Have you engaged with/organised the resources needed? What are they?

REFLECTION

Notes on what worked well and if you hit your target. What do you need to reassess for next week and try again?

WEEKLY TARGET

Date………………..

(Document the "bite sized" pieces of your goal, keep it simple and achievable)

_____

_____

_____

Have you engaged with/organised the resources needed? What are they?

_____

_____

_____

REFLECTION

Notes on what worked well and if you hit your target. What do you need to reassess for next week and try again?

_____

_____

_____

WEEKLY TARGET

Date................

(Document the "bite sized" pieces of your goal, keep it simple and achievable)

_____

_____

_____

_____

Have you engaged with/organised the resources needed? What are they?

_____

_____

_____

_____

REFLECTION

Notes on what worked well and if you hit your target. What do you need to reassess for next week and try again?

_____

_____

_____

_____

WEEKLY TARGET

Date...................

(Document the "bite sized" pieces of your goal, keep it simple and achievable)

Have you engaged with/organised the resources needed? What are they?

REFLECTION

Notes on what worked well and if you hit your target. What do you need to reassess for next week and try again?

WEEKLY TARGET

Date……………..

(Document the "bite sized" pieces of your goal, keep it simple and achievable)

Have you engaged with/organised the resources needed? What are they?

REFLECTION

Notes on what worked well and if you hit your target. What do you need to reassess for next week and try again?

E - Endeavour

What are your goals for your endeavor? Your endeavour is whatever you are working on or your production. It could be your work, business, study, home making or homeschooling etc. What are you wanting to achieve next? Remember to keep your targets specific and achievable.

ANNUAL VISION
(Blue Sky Goal)

90 DAY VISION

PLAN IT

What resources do you need to acquire/use/source to achieve this goal?

What are the potential blockages to achieving this goal? What do you need to be aware of, look out for and prepare to manage?

How will you know you have achieved this goal? What will it look like? Feel like?

REFLECTION

Did you achieve your vision? If not, what got in the way - how can you reassess and try again? Do you need to pivot and shift your goal post? Or do you need to source/use resources more effectively? Do not be discouraged! Change takes time and is often hard, but is so worth it!

90 DAY VISION

PLAN IT

What resources do you need to acquire/use/source to achieve this goal?

What are the potential blockages to achieving this goal? What do you need to be aware of, look out for and prepare to manage?

How will you know you have achieved this goal? What will it look like? Feel like?

REFLECTION

Did you achieve your vision? If not, what got in the way - how can you reassess and try again? Do you need to pivot and shift your goal post? Or do you need to source/use resources more effectively? Do not be discouraged! Change takes time and is often hard, but is so worth it!

90 DAY VISION

PLAN IT

What resources do you need to acquire/use/source to achieve this goal?

What are the potential blockages to achieving this goal? What do you need to be aware of, look out for and prepare to manage?

How will you know you have achieved this goal? What will it look like? Feel like?

REFLECTION

Did you achieve your vision? If not, what got in the way - how can you reassess and try again? Do you need to pivot and shift your goal post? Or do you need to source/use resources more effectively? Do not be discouraged! Change takes time and is often hard, but is so worth it!

90 DAY VISION

PLAN IT

What resources do you need to acquire/use/source to achieve this goal?

What are the potential blockages to achieving this goal? What do you need to be aware of, look out for and prepare to manage?

How will you know you have achieved this goal? What will it look like? Feel like?

REFLECTION

Did you achieve your vision? If not, what got in the way - how can you reassess and try again? Do you need to pivot and shift your goal post? Or do you need to source/use resources more effectively? Do not be discouraged! Change takes time and is often hard, but is so worth it!

_____

_____

_____

_____

_____

_____

_____

_____

_____

_____

_____

_____

_____

WEEKLY TARGET

Date.....................

(Document the "bite sized" pieces of your goal, keep it simple and achievable)

Have you engaged with/organised the resources needed? What are they?

REFLECTION

Notes on what worked well and if you hit your target. What do you need to reassess for next week and try again?

WEEKLY TARGET

Date……………...

(Document the "bite sized" pieces of your goal, keep it simple and achievable)

Have you engaged with/organised the resources needed? What are they?

REFLECTION

Notes on what worked well and if you hit your target. What do you need to reassess for next week and try again?

WEEKLY TARGET

Date……………..

(Document the "bite sized" pieces of your goal, keep it simple and achievable)

Have you engaged with/organised the resources needed? What are they?

REFLECTION

Notes on what worked well and if you hit your target. What do you need to reassess for next week and try again?

WEEKLY TARGET

Date..................

(Document the "bite sized" pieces of your goal, keep it simple and achievable)

Have you engaged with/organised the resources needed? What are they?

REFLECTION

Notes on what worked well and if you hit your target. What do you need to reassess for next week and try again?

WEEKLY TARGET

Date……………..

(Document the "bite sized" pieces of your goal, keep it simple and achievable)

_____

_____

_____

_____

Have you engaged with/organised the resources needed? What are they?

_____

_____

_____

_____

REFLECTION

Notes on what worked well and if you hit your target. What do you need to reassess for next week and try again?

_____

_____

_____

WEEKLY TARGET

Date....................

(Document the "bite sized" pieces of your goal, keep it simple and achievable)

_____

_____

_____

_____

Have you engaged with/organised the resources needed? What are they?

_____

_____

_____

_____

REFLECTION

Notes on what worked well and if you hit your target. What do you need to reassess for next week and try again?

_____

_____

_____

_____

WEEKLY TARGET

Date……………..

(Document the "bite sized" pieces of your goal, keep it simple and achievable)

Have you engaged with/organised the resources needed? What are they?

REFLECTION

Notes on what worked well and if you hit your target. What do you need to reassess for next week and try again?

WEEKLY TARGET

Date……………..

(Document the "bite sized" pieces of your goal, keep it simple and achievable)

_____

_____

_____

_____

Have you engaged with/organised the resources needed? What are they?

_____

_____

_____

_____

REFLECTION

Notes on what worked well and if you hit your target. What do you need to reassess for next week and try again?

_____

_____

_____

WEEKLY TARGET

Date……………..

(Document the "bite sized" pieces of your goal, keep it simple and achievable)

Have you engaged with/organised the resources needed? What are they?

REFLECTION

Notes on what worked well and if you hit your target. What do you need to reassess for next week and try again?

WEEKLY TARGET

Date........................

(Document the "bite sized" pieces of your goal, keep it simple and achievable)

Have you engaged with/organised the resources needed? What are they?

REFLECTION

Notes on what worked well and if you hit your target. What do you need to reassess for next week and try again?

WEEKLY TARGET

Date……………..

(Document the "bite sized" pieces of your goal, keep it simple and achievable)

Have you engaged with/organised the resources needed? What are they?

REFLECTION

Notes on what worked well and if you hit your target. What do you need to reassess for next week and try again?

WEEKLY TARGET

Date……………...

(Document the "bite sized" pieces of your goal, keep it simple and achievable)

Have you engaged with/organised the resources needed? What are they?

REFLECTION

Notes on what worked well and if you hit your target. What do you need to reassess for next week and try again?

WEEKLY TARGET

Date...................

(Document the "bite sized" pieces of your goal, keep it simple and achievable)

_____

_____

_____

_____

Have you engaged with/organised the resources needed? What are they?

_____

_____

_____

REFLECTION

Notes on what worked well and if you hit your target. What do you need to reassess for next week and try again?

_____

_____

_____

WEEKLY TARGET

Date……………..

(Document the "bite sized" pieces of your goal, keep it simple and achievable)

_____

_____

_____

Have you engaged with/organised the resources needed? What are they?

_____

_____

_____

REFLECTION

Notes on what worked well and if you hit your target. What do you need to reassess for next week and try again?

_____

_____

_____

WEEKLY TARGET

Date………………..

(Document the "bite sized" pieces of your goal, keep it simple and achievable)

Have you engaged with/organised the resources needed? What are they?

REFLECTION

Notes on what worked well and if you hit your target. What do you need to reassess for next week and try again?

WEEKLY TARGET

Date……………...

(Document the "bite sized" pieces of your goal, keep it simple and achievable)

....

....

....

Have you engaged with/organised the resources needed? What are they?

....

....

....

....

REFLECTION

Notes on what worked well and if you hit your target. What do you need to reassess for next week and try again?

....

....

....

WEEKLY TARGET

Date………………..

(Document the "bite sized" pieces of your goal, keep it simple and achievable)

Have you engaged with/organised the resources needed? What are they?

REFLECTION

Notes on what worked well and if you hit your target. What do you need to reassess for next week and try again?

WEEKLY TARGET

Date........................

(Document the "bite sized" pieces of your goal, keep it simple and achievable)

Have you engaged with/organised the resources needed? What are they?

REFLECTION

Notes on what worked well and if you hit your target. What do you need to reassess for next week and try again?

WEEKLY TARGET

Date……………….

(Document the "bite sized" pieces of your goal, keep it simple and achievable)

_____

_____

_____

_____

Have you engaged with/organised the resources needed? What are they?

_____

_____

_____

_____

REFLECTION

Notes on what worked well and if you hit your target. What do you need to reassess for next week and try again?

_____

_____

_____

_____

WEEKLY TARGET

Date.....................

(Document the "bite sized" pieces of your goal, keep it simple and achievable)

Have you engaged with/organised the resources needed? What are they?

REFLECTION

Notes on what worked well and if you hit your target. What do you need to reassess for next week and try again?

The Family Legacy Journal

WEEKLY TARGET

Date……………..

(Document the "bite sized" pieces of your goal, keep it simple and achievable)

Have you engaged with/organised the resources needed? What are they?

REFLECTION

Notes on what worked well and if you hit your target. What do you need to reassess for next week and try again?

WEEKLY TARGET

Date………………..

(Document the "bite sized" pieces of your goal, keep it simple and achievable)

Have you engaged with/organised the resources needed? What are they?

REFLECTION

Notes on what worked well and if you hit your target. What do you need to reassess for next week and try again?

WEEKLY TARGET

Date……………..

(Document the "bite sized" pieces of your goal, keep it simple and achievable)

_____

_____

_____

_____

Have you engaged with/organised the resources needed? What are they?

_____

_____

_____

_____

REFLECTION

Notes on what worked well and if you hit your target. What do you need to reassess for next week and try again?

_____

_____

_____

WEEKLY TARGET

Date..................

(Document the "bite sized" pieces of your goal, keep it simple and achievable)

_____

_____

_____

Have you engaged with/organised the resources needed? What are they?

_____

_____

_____

REFLECTION

Notes on what worked well and if you hit your target. What do you need to reassess for next week and try again?

_____

_____

_____

WEEKLY TARGET

Date……………..

(Document the "bite sized" pieces of your goal, keep it simple and achievable)

Have you engaged with/organised the resources needed? What are they?

REFLECTION

Notes on what worked well and if you hit your target. What do you need to reassess for next week and try again?

WEEKLY TARGET

Date……………..

(Document the "bite sized" pieces of your goal, keep it simple and achievable)

Have you engaged with/organised the resources needed? What are they?

REFLECTION

Notes on what worked well and if you hit your target. What do you need to reassess for next week and try again?

WEEKLY TARGET

Date.................

(Document the "bite sized" pieces of your goal, keep it simple and achievable)

Have you engaged with/organised the resources needed? What are they?

REFLECTION

Notes on what worked well and if you hit your target. What do you need to reassess for next week and try again?

WEEKLY TARGET

Date……………..

(Document the "bite sized" pieces of your goal, keep it simple and achievable)

Have you engaged with/organised the resources needed? What are they?

REFLECTION

Notes on what worked well and if you hit your target. What do you need to reassess for next week and try again?

WEEKLY TARGET

Date.................

(Document the "bite sized" pieces of your goal, keep it simple and achievable)

Have you engaged with/organised the resources needed? What are they?

REFLECTION

Notes on what worked well and if you hit your target. What do you need to reassess for next week and try again?

WEEKLY TARGET

Date.....................

(Document the "bite sized" pieces of your goal, keep it simple and achievable)

_____

_____

_____

Have you engaged with/organised the resources needed? What are they?

_____

_____

_____

REFLECTION

Notes on what worked well and if you hit your target. What do you need to reassess for next week and try again?

_____

_____

_____

WEEKLY TARGET

Date.................

(Document the "bite sized" pieces of your goal, keep it simple and achievable)

_____

_____

_____

_____

Have you engaged with/organised the resources needed? What are they?

_____

_____

_____

_____

REFLECTION

Notes on what worked well and if you hit your target. What do you need to reassess for next week and try again?

_____

_____

_____

WEEKLY TARGET

Date……………..

(Document the "bite sized" pieces of your goal, keep it simple and achievable)

_____

_____

_____

_____

Have you engaged with/organised the resources needed? What are they?

_____

_____

_____

_____

REFLECTION

Notes on what worked well and if you hit your target. What do you need to reassess for next week and try again?

_____

_____

_____

_____

WEEKLY TARGET

Date……………..

(Document the "bite sized" pieces of your goal, keep it simple and achievable)

⎯⎯

⎯⎯

⎯⎯

Have you engaged with/organised the resources needed? What are they?

⎯⎯

⎯⎯

⎯⎯

REFLECTION

Notes on what worked well and if you hit your target. What do you need to reassess for next week and try again?

⎯⎯

⎯⎯

⎯⎯

WEEKLY TARGET

Date................

(Document the "bite sized" pieces of your goal, keep it simple and achievable)

Have you engaged with/organised the resources needed? What are they?

REFLECTION

Notes on what worked well and if you hit your target. What do you need to reassess for next week and try again?

WEEKLY TARGET

Date……………..

(Document the "bite sized" pieces of your goal, keep it simple and achievable)

Have you engaged with/organised the resources needed? What are they?

REFLECTION

Notes on what worked well and if you hit your target. What do you need to reassess for next week and try again?

WEEKLY TARGET

Date.....................

(Document the "bite sized" pieces of your goal, keep it simple and achievable)

Have you engaged with/organised the resources needed? What are they?

REFLECTION

Notes on what worked well and if you hit your target. What do you need to reassess for next week and try again?

WEEKLY TARGET

Date................

(Document the "bite sized" pieces of your goal, keep it simple and achievable)

_____
_____
_____
_____

Have you engaged with/organised the resources needed? What are they?

_____
_____
_____
_____

REFLECTION

Notes on what worked well and if you hit your target. What do you need to reassess for next week and try again?

_____
_____
_____

WEEKLY TARGET

Date……………..

(Document the "bite sized" pieces of your goal, keep it simple and achievable)

Have you engaged with/organised the resources needed? What are they?

REFLECTION

Notes on what worked well and if you hit your target. What do you need to reassess for next week and try again?

WEEKLY TARGET

Date……………..

(Document the "bite sized" pieces of your goal, keep it simple and achievable)

Have you engaged with/organised the resources needed? What are they?

REFLECTION

Notes on what worked well and if you hit your target. What do you need to reassess for next week and try again?

WEEKLY TARGET

Date................

(Document the "bite sized" pieces of your goal, keep it simple and achievable)

Have you engaged with/organised the resources needed? What are they?

REFLECTION

Notes on what worked well and if you hit your target. What do you need to reassess for next week and try again?

WEEKLY TARGET

Date……………..

(Document the "bite sized" pieces of your goal, keep it simple and achievable)

_____

_____

_____

Have you engaged with/organised the resources needed? What are they?

_____

_____

_____

REFLECTION

Notes on what worked well and if you hit your target. What do you need to reassess for next week and try again?

_____

_____

_____

The Family Legacy Journal

WEEKLY TARGET

Date……………...

(Document the "bite sized" pieces of your goal, keep it simple and achievable)

Have you engaged with/organised the resources needed? What are they?

REFLECTION

Notes on what worked well and if you hit your target. What do you need to reassess for next week and try again?

WEEKLY TARGET

Date………………..

(Document the "bite sized" pieces of your goal, keep it simple and achievable)

_____

_____

_____

_____

Have you engaged with/organised the resources needed? What are they?

_____

_____

_____

_____

REFLECTION

Notes on what worked well and if you hit your target. What do you need to reassess for next week and try again?

_____

_____

_____

WEEKLY TARGET

Date……………..

(Document the "bite sized" pieces of your goal, keep it simple and achievable)

Have you engaged with/organised the resources needed? What are they?

REFLECTION

Notes on what worked well and if you hit your target. What do you need to reassess for next week and try again?

WEEKLY TARGET

Date..................

(Document the "bite sized" pieces of your goal, keep it simple and achievable)

Have you engaged with/organised the resources needed? What are they?

REFLECTION

Notes on what worked well and if you hit your target. What do you need to reassess for next week and try again?

WEEKLY TARGET

Date.....................

(Document the "bite sized" pieces of your goal, keep it simple and achievable)

Have you engaged with/organised the resources needed? What are they?

REFLECTION

Notes on what worked well and if you hit your target. What do you need to reassess for next week and try again?

The Family Legacy Journal

WEEKLY TARGET

Date……………..

(Document the "bite sized" pieces of your goal, keep it simple and achievable)

Have you engaged with/organised the resources needed? What are they?

REFLECTION

Notes on what worked well and if you hit your target. What do you need to reassess for next week and try again?

WEEKLY TARGET

Date...................

(Document the "bite sized" pieces of your goal, keep it simple and achievable)

_____

_____

_____

Have you engaged with/organised the resources needed? What are they?

_____

_____

_____

REFLECTION

Notes on what worked well and if you hit your target. What do you need to reassess for next week and try again?

_____

_____

_____

WEEKLY TARGET

Date......................

(Document the "bite sized" pieces of your goal, keep it simple and achievable)

Have you engaged with/organised the resources needed? What are they?

REFLECTION

Notes on what worked well and if you hit your target. What do you need to reassess for next week and try again?

WEEKLY TARGET

Date……………..

(Document the "bite sized" pieces of your goal, keep it simple and achievable)

_____
_____
_____

_____

Have you engaged with/organised the resources needed? What are they?

_____
_____
_____

_____

REFLECTION

Notes on what worked well and if you hit your target. What do you need to reassess for next week and try again?

_____
_____
_____

WEEKLY TARGET

Date.....................

(Document the "bite sized" pieces of your goal, keep it simple and achievable)

Have you engaged with/organised the resources needed? What are they?

REFLECTION

Notes on what worked well and if you hit your target. What do you need to reassess for next week and try again?

WEEKLY TARGET

Date……………..

(Document the "bite sized" pieces of your goal, keep it simple and achievable)

Have you engaged with/organised the resources needed? What are they?

REFLECTION

Notes on what worked well and if you hit your target. What do you need to reassess for next week and try again?

Daily Affirmation List

Every morning when you wake up and wander into the bathroom and see yourself in the mirror for the first time that day, you might think something along the lines of:

"gosh I look tired", or "I wish I had more sleep". Perhaps you think, "When did I get so grey?"

Negative self-talk is not going to help you step into the new day with confidence and it is a habit most of us need to break.

You are going to start telling yourself *helpful* and *wonderful* things each morning. Create a list of affirmations that you find helpful, uplifting and empowering. You may have seen them on my page, or others. You may have heard them in a podcast or seen them in an advertisement, you may have read them in your Bible. Curate a collection of inspirational affirmations that help you achieve your vision.

The Family Legacy Journal

Moments that are Memories to Keep...

Take note of any funny, dear or inspiring moments you experienced with your family. Some moments are worth writing down to read and smile over for years to come.

The Family Legacy Journal

Calendar to Mark Milestones

Use this calendar to mark any notable milestones you want to hold onto. For example, did your teen choose to attend family dinner after refusing for months? Did your child say "I love you" for the first time recently? Did you and your spouse/partner really connect whilst on a date? Did you take a weekend away to build family connection? Did you hit that goal weight or get that pay rise? All these moments run the risk of being washed downstream as time marches on, let me encourage you to document these milestones and hold onto them forever.

Month _____

Sunday	Monday	Tuesday	Wednesday	Thursday	Friday	Saturday

Month _____

Sunday	Monday	Tuesday	Wednesday	Thursday	Friday	Saturday

Month _____

Sunday	Monday	Tuesday	Wednesday	Thursday	Friday	Saturday

Month _____

Sunday	Monday	Tuesday	Wednesday	Thursday	Friday	Saturday

Month _____

Sunday	Monday	Tuesday	Wednesday	Thursday	Friday	Saturday

Month _____

Sunday	Monday	Tuesday	Wednesday	Thursday	Friday	Saturday

Month _____

	Sunday	Monday	Tuesday	Wednesday	Thursday	Friday	Saturday

Month _____

Sunday	Monday	Tuesday	Wednesday	Thursday	Friday	Saturday

Month _____

Sunday	Monday	Tuesday	Wednesday	Thursday	Friday	Saturday

Month _____

Sunday	Monday	Tuesday	Wednesday	Thursday	Friday	Saturday

Month _____

Sunday	Monday	Tuesday	Wednesday	Thursday	Friday	Saturday

Month _____

Sunday	Monday	Tuesday	Wednesday	Thursday	Friday	Saturday

Books, Resources and Notable Quotes

Has someone told you about a great book, podcast or resource? Write it down here. Use this page to keep track of your inspiration, education and resources.

The Family Legacy Journal

Notes

www.ingramcontent.com/pod-product-compliance
Lightning Source LLC
Chambersburg PA
CBHW072151200426
43209CB00052B/1109